MW00416630

Heaven Talks Back

an uncommon conversation

Jon Macks

Introduction by Jay Leno

Simon & Schuster

SIMON & SCHUSTER
Rockefeller Center
1230 Avenue of the Americas
New York, NY 10020

Simon & Schuster and colophon are
registered trademarks of Simon & Schuster Inc.

Designed by Chris Welch
Manufactured in the United States of America

1   3   5   7   9   10   8   6   4   2

Library of Congress Cataloging-in-Publication Data
Macks, Jon.
Heaven talks back : an uncommon conversation / Jon Macks ;
introduction by Jay Leno
p.   cm.
1. God—Humor. 2. Conduct of life—Humor. I. Title.
PN6231.P3M32   1998
818'.5402—dc21   98-37843
CIP
ISBN 0-684-85272-1

≽ Acknowledgments ≼

To David Rosenthal and Marysue Rucci, who helped create and hone this book and make it a reality.

To Jay Leno, James Carville, David Steinberg, Billy Crystal, Don Mischer and Bob O'Donnell—they are more than mentors, they are cherished friends.

To Fang, who has been a "best man" in every sense of the word.

To Jay, James, the Haskells, the Bentons, the Kromnicks and all the people of Agoura and Oak Park, who came through for Julie and me when we really needed some help.

To Jack Dytman, Bob Myman and Howard Silverstein, who look out for my financial and career interests.

To the inventor of Viagra anti-impotence medicine.

ACKNOWLEDGMENTS

To Dave Esola, Bob Caruso, Doug Warrick, Mary Matalin, Paul Begala, Herb Kohl, Tom Oppel, Michael Matthews, Ray Mabus and Tony Peist, all of whom have made a difference in my life.

To my parents and my brother, Adam, who will be so happy at this acknowledgment that they will pledge two thousand dollars to plant some trees in Israel.

To Jodie Foster and our love child.

To the Malibu Mustangs baseball team.

And to God, without whom this book and the entire existence of the cosmos would not be possible.

To Julie, Daniel, Samantha and Ricky

⨠ Introduction by Jay Leno ⨜

When I was a kid, I used to read about how Bob Hope had a group of writers he could call at 3:00 A.M., tell what he needed the next day and by morning they would have dozens of jokes on his desk. As I got older and began my career, I always thought how great that would be, to work with a writer so inventive and creative that he could instantly find the humor in any situation. I was lucky enough to find someone like that—Jon Macks.

Jon's output is legendary—he writes a hundred jokes a day, every day, on every imaginable topic. And he does this while creating brilliant comedy sketches; providing speech material for Bill Clinton, Bob Dole, Al Gore and NBC executives; contributing to *George* magazine;

script doctoring; creating comedy albums; working on the past four Emmy telecasts and writing for Billy Crystal on the last two Academy Award shows. The reason his talents are in demand? Jon has the ability of all great comedy writers: to find the odd link between two topics, to twist the normal into the absurd and to see, in every situation, what is stupid, odd or out of place.

And he's not afraid to admit that he's been Touched by God.

I'll be honest, a lot of people were surprised when they found out Jon had been talking to God. And, of course, this revelation confused everyone at NBC—half the people here thought he meant Jack Welch, half thought he meant Jerry Seinfeld. But I knew who Jon was referring to, which is why I asked if he could put in a good word and see if God would come on *The Tonight Show* as a guest. We've been trying to book him for years. Jon told me God was very flattered but had to decline—he was too busy rejecting the pleas of sports fans praying that their local team would win the latest game.

I hope you get to meet Jon in person one day. Because

once you get past his newfound religious zeal, the beatific look he has and his nonstop speaking in tongues, you'll find a sharp, funny writer with Hall of Fame credentials. And if you believe for a second that all those other channelers out there may have had divine conversations, then you have to think there's a chance Jon had some too.

It would be presumptuous of me to say that God needs any help with his work, but if God did feel the need to punch up his material and give it an edge, he'd do what I do—turn to Jon Macks, the best comedy writer of his generation.

"God works in a mysterious way."

— T. S. Eliot, *"The Hippopotamus"*

⇒ Heaven Talks Back ⇐

an uncommon conversation

When I was a child, my mother used to say, "God is always with you, God is your best friend." Then she ran off with our minister, leaving behind me, my father, a younger brother and my new best friend, the Almighty.

As you can imagine, I began to have doubts; doubts about faith, questions about how a loving, caring Supreme Being could allow my mother to do this. I never stopped believing in God, I just refused to believe that God was interested in my life.

Then in February of 1997 I had an experience that changed all that. God began to speak to me. Personally. It was February 28. I know that because I wrote it down on a Post-it Note so I wouldn't forget the date. We entered into a rather extensive dialogue. Actually it was more of a monologue; God isn't a very good listener. To be honest, if you met him at work, you'd think of him as a know-it-all type. Lasting a full year, our exchanges became a book. We call it *Heaven Talks Back*.

These are God's own words. Sometimes he spoke in the third person, other times in the first person. Since he's God, he can speak in the fourth person if he wants. The God that spoke to me is not the forgiving God the charlatans of today would have you believe, nor is he offering friendship to humankind. Think of him more like your supervisor at work—shallow, self-centered, sometimes willing to help but, more often than not, letting things go wrong so he can bitch about the outcome. All in all, God is one moody, unpredictable and easily pissed-off Supreme Being. That is the God I would like all of us to know. Before it is too late.

January 1

I did not create Man in my image. Unless you look like Charlton Heston and sound like James Earl Jones. Women created in my image tend to look like Elle MacPherson, although not quite as tall.

January 2

I'm there to help. But let's get something straight.
I have 100 million galaxies to take care of. I
don't have time to help some spoiled pituitary freaks
win the Super Bowl. So stop praying for my help in
the locker room. It just pisses me off.

January 4

A true master is not the one with the most students, but the one who creates the most masters. I read that in a fortune cookie once.

January 6

There are some who believe that people never die, that they simply change form. They are in for a big surprise.

January 11

God asks only that you include yourself among those you love because self-love is the key to happiness. But too much self-love can make you go blind.

January 12

⚕

There is no such thing as sin. Or maybe there is. It's for me to know and you to find out.

January 13

G od's tip for the day: When playing blackjack, always split aces, eights and nines.

January 16

The first thing to understand about the universe is that no condition is "good" or "bad." It's more of a one-to-ten scale, ten being the best, one being the worst. For example, after a tough day, an ice-cold Bombay Sapphire, olive on the side, is a ten. Fat-free potato chips—a one. Plus they give me gas.

January 18

𝄪

Y ou are not my spiritual offspring. I don't care how many times you pray to "God our Father," I'm not your dad. My purpose in creating you was simply for amusement. So cut the crap about being in my image. Consider yourselves action figures.

January 20

No one who has attained mastery is dull. Except for the people on PBS and anyone from England.

January 21

God's little insight: Who came up with the idea that no two snowflakes are alike?

Of course they're alike. It's an assembly line up here—five, maybe six basic molds. We just churn them out.

If we had time, sure, we'd give each snowflake individual attention. But those days are gone—everything up here is mass-produced.

January 24

/I\

You should spend a lot more time enjoying life on earth and a lot less time worrying about getting to heaven.

It's no picnic up here. You can't believe the paperwork. And it was supposed to get a lot easier with Windows 95. Nothing but problems. Half the angels are Mac, half are Windows. Here I am, the Supreme Being in the universe, and I can't get anyone to service our computers. And nobody knows what the hell is going to happen when the date changes to January 1, 2000.

January 28

Every heart earnestly asks, "Which is the path to God?"

There are many true paths. But just for fun, I put in one false path. One of your religions, and I'm not saying which one, is way off. Its followers are on the highway to hell. And no, I won't give you a hint.

February 1

God's tip of the day: Always buy a new car at the end of the month. The salesmen have quotas and you get a better deal. I know, it's February 1; I should have told you January 28. It slipped my mind. Like new wheels for you are the only things I have to worry about. Selfish bastards.

February 2

Your teachers have told you of an angry God, a jealous God, a God who needs to be touched. How the hell do they know?

February 3

⁄⁀

The prophets say it is man's first nature to be unconditionally loving. But just in case, there's no-fault divorce.

February 6

God's little insight: Exhibition games are meaningless. I remember one year, the Yankees were 9 and 18 down in Florida and won ninety-eight games during the regular season, then swept the Phillies in four. But that was before all these play-off games. And don't get me started on the wild card. Nowadays it's just for television.

February 7

⋏⋏

Never look back with regret. Although if I had to do it all over again, I'd have made Napoleon a bit taller. If he'd been just 5'4", he'd never have had that complex.

A lot of short guys are like that. Small of stature, big of ego. Look at Dustin Hoffman. Even worse, look at Ross Perot.

February 8

The universe is in perfect symmetry. Men have two hands, women have two breasts. Come on, it was a joke! Ever since Anita Hill, you can't kid anybody.

February 9

⁂

You are, have always been and will always be a divine part of the divine whole. Still, you can never have too much term life insurance.

February 10

Every question has an answer. Everything can be explained. Except the popularity of Yanni.

February 12

I have given you nothing shameful, least of all your very body and its functions. However, if you weigh over 325 pounds, try not to wear shorts.

February 13

There are those who say you must overcome your desires. I say you must simply change them. Unless you're president of the United States—then you can get away with anything.

February 14

At the critical juncture in all relationships, there is only one question: What would love do now? The correct answer—buy flowers, shmuck, it's Valentine's Day. And don't believe her for a second when she says, "You don't have to buy me flowers this year." You better buy them. What is it, eighty dollars? For guaranteed sex that night. You spent a lot more at bars when you were single on nights you completely struck out. Trust me, I saw it all.

February 20

G od's tip of the day: If your current boyfriend asks how he is in bed compared to your ex, lie. Lie, lie lie! Completely forget about the thou-shalt-not-lie commandment. That was only intended for politicians and telemarketers, and look what good that did me. So just lie. Why cause yourself aggravation down the road? Life's too short.

February 23

⁄⁀⁀

At the root of every problem is the fact that you do not consider yourself worthy to be spoken to by God. Is it the God-is-infallible thing? Well, if it's any consolation, there have been a few foul-ups. Nothing deliberate, just mix-ups in communications. For example, *Atlanta* was supposed to sink into the sea, not *Atlantis*. It would have saved Braves fans a lot of agita. And Marisa Tomei was never supposed to win Best Supporting Actress for *My Cousin Vinny.* I mean, come on, nice girl and cute, but she's Sandra Bullock lite. Turns out Price Waterhouse counted her votes twice by accident.

February 27

HEY YOU! TRYING TO READ THIS FOR FREE IN THE BOOKSTORE INSTEAD OF BUYING IT! DON'T PRETEND YOU'RE JUST SKIMMING. YOU'RE UP TO FEBRUARY 27 ALREADY! YOU WANT A COMMANDMENT, HERE'S A COMMANDMENT: PUT IT DOWN OR BUY IT!

February 28

Laughter is the currency of heaven. But you would think my people here would have more important things to do than send E-mail. I come in every morning, and I've got thirty messages with the latest Monica Lewinsky jokes. Although I have to admit, I never thought Jewish girls did that.

March 1

G od's little insight: Buy Intel.

March 3

⋀⋀

I gave your spirit a physical body for you to pro-create and enjoy the pleasures of the sensual. Just one small favor: Don't scream out my name during sex. It can get very annoying, all those voices yelling. Try calling out the name of your partner. If you're having sex without a partner, scream out the name of that month's Playmate or the battery company. "Miss October!" or "Yes, yes, yes Duracell!" And another thing—gerbils are one of my creatures. Leave them alone.

March 4

No prayer goes unanswered.* It just takes me a while to get around to it. Hey, I'm one guy. You ask for help, it goes into the pile. Eventually I get to it. Sometimes by the time I get to your request, you're dead.

*But remember what I said on January 2. Don't bother me about sports.

March 7

If a thing is so obviously right, just do it. It really ticks me off that I come up with these pearls and some ad hack from Portland rips it off and makes it a slogan for Nike. Like Nikes really make you a better athlete. Put a pair of Buster Brown wing tips on Michael Jordan and he still scores forty-five over Brent Barry in Nikes.

March 12

The people who have the "faith to move mountains" and die six weeks later should be content that they have moved mountains for six weeks. But they never are. They're the worst complainers when they get here, all that talk about how they got gypped. I give them two weeks to knock it off, then I let them burn in hell.

March 16

I have a plan for each and every one of you. The problem is, the last time I merged files, I lost it.

March 17

You are in a partnership with God. Each of us has responsibilities in this cosmic partnership. On your end, you need to follow the Commandments, tend to my pastures, protect the earth and follow the Golden Rule. I sit back and take the credit.

March 18

Love thy neighbor. And hope her husband doesn't come home early.

March 20

God's tip of the day: This is important advice with spring just around the corner. No matter how warm it is, never wear white before Memorial Day. The only ones who can wear white all year long are angels, Elvis impersonators and Jimmy Swaggart.

March 23

ᐱᐱ

God's tip for women: Don't believe him when he says it's just a cold sore. In fact, don't believe men about anything. They lie about how much money they make, they lie about how they scored the winning touchdown in high school, they lie about their height, they lie about lying. They are incapable of telling the truth. And they lie especially about anything involving numbers. Here's a good formula—whenever a man gives you his golf score or genital size, add fifteen or subtract two. Don't ask me to explain how it works, it just does.

March 25

You do not need to see God to know that he exists. You want proof—here. Think of a number between one and nine. Multiply it by nine. Take the two integers in what you came up with and add them together. Take that number and subtract five. Take the number you have left and write down the corresponding letter of the alphabet (for example, if the number is seven you would think of G). Think of a country that begins with the letter you wrote down. Take the second letter in the name of that country and think of an animal that begins with that letter. Is it an elephant in Denmark?

How much more proof do you want?

March 27

I am always with you. I am always with everybody. This is a hard concept for most people to imagine, so let me try to explain. Remember in the first *Superman* movie where the missile is going to blow up the house of Valerie Perrine's mother at the same time the earthquake is about to swallow up Lois? Superman had to let Lois get killed because he couldn't be in two places at once. Well, on my worst day, I'm better than Superman.

March 31

Expectations ruin relationships. So if you want a good relationship with me, don't expect too much.

April 1

I'm going to test your faith. Just like I did with Abraham and Isaac. If you do this, I promise you eternity. Go upstairs in your house. If you don't have an upstairs, build one. Take off all your clothes, get a Magic Marker, make a cross and the Star of David on your chest. Very important—the cross should be on the left, the star on the right. Now go outside and face east. In a loud voice shout, "God is good." Have you done this? April fool!

April 3

D o you set the clocks ahead an hour this weekend or back an hour? I can never keep that
straight.

April 4

Do you imagine that God does not enjoy a good joke? I tell you, God invented humor. Here, I'll prove it. "Two Jews walk into a bar. They buy it."

April 7

⚕

When a person is in a really deep sleep, you have to shake him a little. This is not an allegory. I mean it exactly as I said it. Go over and shake him. If that doesn't wake him up, chances are he's dead.

April 11

Remember the plan I had for each and every one of you, the one that got lost? Good news—I had a backup disk. Let me explain what I mean by my plan. My plan for Helen Hunt is that she is beautiful, smart, popular and makes $1 million a week. My plan is that you are plain, boring and get audited by the IRS. There is a plan and in it you get screwed. Life isn't fair.

April 14

It is said that true masters are those who have chosen to make a life, rather than make a living. That sounds like something you hear from somebody who's unemployed. You know the type—twenty-four, still at home, sitting in Starbucks all day spewing forth crap about wanting to be fulfilled with their career. Hey, fulfillment doesn't pay the rent. Get a job!

April 15

G od's tip of the day: If you're short of documentation for the deductions on your 1040, slip a cab driver a twenty and he'll generally give you his entire receipt book.

April 19

Did anyone ever think that maybe I have needs? Did any of you ever stop your constant whining and begging for favors for one second and ask, "Is there anything I can do for God?" Don't get me wrong, it's nice being worshiped; it's just that you humans always have an ulterior motive. When do I ever hear from you unless you want something? Never. Just once I'd like to have someone make a sacrifice or a burnt offering without immediately following up with a demand. Surprise me this weekend.

April 20

Fear is the opposite of everything you are. I have no idea what that means.

April 24

Man is Man and God is God. So what the hell is with this cloning of sheep? Do you think the rams like this? It pretty much cuts them out of the fun loop. Have you ever looked at a ram from down low and behind? There's a reason I made them like that: so they could have sex and have lots of little sheep the way I planned it. You want to play God? Be my guest, it's all yours. Guaranteed, two weeks on the job, you quit from all the aggravation.

April 26

God has five attitudes: totally joyful, loving, accepting, blessing and grateful. That's on a good day.

On a bad day I have just one attitude—really, really pissed off. Like the day I turned Lot's wife into a pillar of salt. I admit it, I overreacted; and ever since then, sodomy has had a bad connotation. Ridiculous!

April 30

"All you need is love." I hate those lyrics. If love is all you need, how come I had to listen to John Lennon badmouth Paul every day? "I was the genius, he was the pretty boy." If he was such a genius, how come he ended up married to Yoko and dead, while Paul got his knighthood and is still alive? Bad as the two of them were, it's nothing compared to the gossip and backstabbing up here. And if you think there are suck-ups on earth, wait till you see the jockeying around old Mr. Supreme Being. If you get here.

May 1

God's tip of the day: Always turn in the direction of the skid. I know this is a better tip for the winter months but I forgot. So sue me.

May 3

If you think you are right about everything you are not God. You are Donald Trump.

May 5

My messages will come in a hundred forms. You would think that we could integrate our communications systems up here but we can't, so just put up with it.

May 7

God's little insight: If you see a woman with tiny arms, a thin waist and huge breasts, chances are she's got implants. A doctor told me that— something about ratio of fat content. You learn something new every day.

May 8

If God is your target, you're in luck, because God is so big you can't miss him. Although with summer coming up, I may go on Jenny Craig to lose a few pounds.

May 10

⚡

God's tip of the day: The movie sequel is never as good as the original. Never. Just forget about even renting one.

May 15

What you fear, you attract. Fortunately there are anti-stalking laws.

May 16

God's tip of the day: If you're at a fancy restaurant, don't fill up on bread.

May 20

I gave you the gift of sex to be used for the purest joy and highest ecstasy. This is true throughout the universe, except in LA, where it can also be used to land a part in a movie.

May 27

Let's be real—you have limits. And the sooner you quit fooling yourself, the better off you'll be. You can't last ten seconds in the ring with Mike Tyson or manage a baseball game better than Bobby Cox or make foul shots better than Shaq. That's just the alcohol talking.

May 30

Never be daunted, because all conditions are temporary. Except herpes. I've got news for you—it's never just a cold sore.

June 1

G od's tip of the day: Never piss off a postal worker. Even I have no idea what sets them off.

June 2

Most people enter marriage with an eye toward what they can get out of it. Women want stability, companionship, a soul mate and love in its deepest purest sense. Men want sex without having to buy dinner first.

June 6

I don't communicate by words alone. Lately I've been using E-mail. My address is GOD@aol.com.

June 9

⁂

You can be your own rule maker. If you want to collect money on Free Parking in Monopoly even though the official rules don't mention it, go ahead, it's no sweat off my back. If you don't consider oral sex as adultery, fine. Like I can be bothered with every little thing that goes on.

June 11

✦

God's little insight: I exaggerated back on March 27. I am technically not "everywhere." I have a couple of body doubles who fill in for me during the busy season.

June 13

All human actions are motivated by one of three things: fear, love or the desire to slow down the aging process.

June 15

God's joke of the week: How many White House interns does it take to screw in a light bulb? None—the president likes it in the dark.

June 17

There is silent spiritual communication from God and there is silent practical communication from God. Spiritual is the quiet moment in your heart of hearts when you feel my divine warmth envelop you. Practical communication is when I telepathically let you know that your date is a psycho and to get the hell out of there.

June 23

Not to decide is to decide. And vice versa.

June 25

I tell you, you can speak to me as if I were your best friend. That's best friend, not doctor. Which means I want to hear gossip, not the latest update on your prostate. Some of you old people, your prayers are like a reading of *Gray's Anatomy.* And please, a little less wailing at the Wailing Wall.

June 30

There is no sweeter sound to my ears than that of humanity rejoicing in song and dance. Although I don't quite get this Lord of the Dance guy. I never like anyone who waxes his chest.

July 1

⁂

God's tip of the day: If you're at the beach with your wife or girlfriend and she catches you checking out a hot babe in a bikini, immediately shake your head in disgust and say, "Look at those, they're not real."

July 2

You should pray every day, not in supplication, but in gratitude for all you have been given. Hey, I'm just like everybody else, I like a little appreciation now and then. Nothing big, no plaques, just a nice "Hey God, good job today."

July 6

Human beings consist of three different energies: fast, slow and government worker.

July 8

God's little insight: I wish I were half as infallible as Martha Stewart thinks she is.

July 12

You may ask, How could God judge God's own creation and call it bad? Easy—everyone makes mistakes. Do you really think I wanted the Black Hole of Calcutta to turn out that way? Do you think I started out by saying, "Hmm, what India needs is a city with cholera, substandard housing and syphilitic lepers begging for scraps from uncaring members of the ruling class"? It would have been better if I just gave them Levittown.

July 16

G od's tip of the day: If you're in a rotisserie baseball league, never take a Colorado Rockies
pitcher.

July 17

⁂

There are a million aspects to me. A billion, a trillion. I am the Sybil of the universe. I have more personalities than Kathie Lee during a hot flash.

July 20

Experience is the result of poor judgment. Poor judgment is the result of lack of experience. So experience equals lack of experience. And you wonder why no one can make a living as a philosophy major.

July 22

People should make a living doing what they love best. So if you love killing people, become a mob hit man or a tobacco company executive.

July 23

To some the glass is half empty, to others the glass is half full. To the busboy, either way, it needs to be cleared.

July 25

The way to reduce pain associated with earthly experiences and events is to change the way you behold them. Good solid advice for you, but frankly, it never works for me. Look, I'm 5 billion years old—do you know how many annual physicals that is? And no matter how many times I try to approach them with a good attitude, I hate having my prostate checked. But I've got to—you can't imagine my health insurance costs.

July 28

/↑\

The voice within is the loudest voice with which I speak. But I must be on a different frequency than most of you because nobody seems to hear me. And the ones who do claim to hear my voice in their heads also tend to hear Elvis and aliens from Area 51.

July 30

What is my greatest creation? Some say it is Man. Others say it is the perfection of a single red rose. Still others believe it is the cosmos in all its splendor. Personally, I think it's the Victoria's Secret catalog. It's the one thing both men and women like to read.

July 31

What gender is God? I am what I am. I am neither male nor female. So technically, you are not in my image, Michael Jackson is.

August 1

God's tip of the day: It's not true that a woman over thirty has a better chance of getting killed by a terrorist than she has of getting married. Totally made up. However, if you're a single woman over thirty-two—how can I put this nicely—you can cancel your subscription to *Bride's* magazine.

August 2

𝄞

The human soul cries out to know—is there a hell?

I think that's on a "need to know" basis and you're not on that list. So before you decide whether to misbehave, do not think of my words, think of the words of the prophet Clint Eastwood: "Do you feel lucky today? Do you, punk?"

August 3

God's little insight: Contrary to popular belief, the French do not worship Jerry Lewis. They find him as insufferable as the rest of us.

August 4

Y ou don't get as many chances as you want. Who do you think you are—Shirley MacLaine? You get one shot, so get it right. And if you screw up, hope that I'm busy that day and don't notice.

August 7

T here are those who interpret my message to be this: Act before you think. Oh, there's a good idea. Can you imagine if everyone did that? Picture four cars at a four-way stop sign. All four drivers refuse to think and just act. Chaos. Pure chaos. Act before you think? If you're the type who acts before she thinks, better get Norplant.

August 10

⚡

Those who pretend to hear my voice say that all bad things that happen are of your choosing.

This is typical—blame the victim. How about blaming the criminal for once? I knew this was going to happen once the Democrats took over in the sixties. Believe me, at my age and with all my property, I'm a Republican.

August 12

God's joke of the week: The pope, a rabbi and Donald Trump were in an airplane. The plane started to crash and there were only two parachutes. The pope said, "Give me one of the parachutes, because I must live to tend to my flock of millions." The rabbi said, "Give me a parachute, because my people have suffered enough." While the two of them were arguing, Donald Trump took all the parachutes and screwed them both. I love that joke.

August 15

Your life's work is a statement of who you are. Which has got to be really depressing for sanitation workers. Or proctologists.

August 16

⁂

One of the mysteries even I can't explain: How come if there's a tornado, it always hits a trailer park? Just living your life as white trash should be suffering enough.

August 17

⁂

Doing is a function of the body. Being is a function of the soul.

For saying this kind of crap, Tony Robbins makes a hundred thousand dollars a day.

August 18

Your life is a script that has already been written. If you're attractive and blonde, that script is *Melrose Place*. If you're like most people, that script is *America's Funniest Home Videos*.

August 20

You ask me, "What is eternity?"
And I answer thusly: Eternity is like watching *The English Patient* in slow motion. On a hard seat. And you have to go to the bathroom the entire time.

August 24

The soul conceives, the mind creates, the body experiences. Although it would have made a lot more sense to have the body conceive, the mind experience and the soul create. It was right at the end of the seventh day creating the universe and I had to hurry. Looking back, I would have done it differently.

August 27

There is only one reason to do anything. It's when somebody bigger than you makes you do it.

September 1

God's tip of the day: Vacation rental prices at the beach really drop after Labor Day. The weather is just as warm, there's no crowd and you can save a bundle.

September 3

🙏

Do not resist that which is placed in front of your eyes. Which is exactly what Bill Clinton told Paula Jones.

September 4

⋏

Your birth is simply a sign that the journey has begun. For some, that journey will be a ride at the beach with the top down. For others it will be a slow rush-hour commute through a detour on Interstate 405.

September 6

Another one of the mysteries even I can't explain: why nubile seventeen-year-old trailer-park blondes with amazing bodies suddenly turn into overweight Jerry Springer fans in polyester stretch pants at age twenty-four.

September 7

A ll people are special and all moments are golden.

Good idea in theory, but let me carry it out to its next logical step: What a golden moment that was for that special person O.J. when he killed two people. I should have known right from the minute Cain killed Abel that the whole concept of special people and a forgiving God was a mistake. Well, just you wait until the new millennium. There's going to be a big shake-up in the earth personnel department. And let's just say there's going to be some massive layoffs.

September 10

God's tip of the day: Next Tuesday, play these numbers in the pick-six lottery: 1, 11, 27, 29, 37, 38. Don't ask me why, I've got a hunch.

September 15

My intention is for you not to fail. So if you fail, it's your fault, not mine.

September 19

There's "enough." For now. But you can anticipate huge shortages in the future. And don't expect me to do anything about it. I'm still pissed *Seinfeld* went off the air.

September 23

A nother one of the mysteries even I can't explain: Why did David Caruso leave *NYPD Blue*? I see people make decisions like that, it makes me sorry I gave you free will.

September 25

The second most difficult thing for people to do is to hear their own souls. The most difficult thing for women to do is to pass by a department store without spending money. The most difficult thing for men to do is to look a woman with a size-38D chest in the eyes.

September 28

The prophets claim that on the day of reckoning I will raise the dead. What am I, David Copperfield? You think Armageddon is a ten-dollar cover, two-drink minimum, everyone watch God do a few tricks? Let me explain something: If you want to see the dead rise, take two Viagra.

September 30

For those who are tired, you have two choices—follow me and my word or try a double latte. The difference is, following me doesn't cost $3.95 at Starbucks.

October 1

God's tip for the baseball playoffs: In a short series, bet on the team with the pitching.

October 3

There are three things beyond human understanding: the magnificence of creation, the ultimate fate of the universe and the relationship of the Clintons.

October 4

God talks to everyone yet is not always understood. A lot like the early Bob Dylan.

October 5

Listen to your feelings and forget the words of others because words are the least reliable purveyors of truth. Especially if written by a lawyer.

October 6

God's tip of the day: If you order a martini and get the olives on the side, you end up with about an eighth of an ounce extra gin. I read that in a James Bond book.

October 11

All of you are special. But attractive people are more special than others.

October 14

⁂

Achievements of the body are meaningless to the soul. But without the body, the soul would not have much fun. Face it: Which would you rather have, the soul of Pamela Anderson in the body of Mother Teresa or the soul of Mother Teresa in the body of Pamela Anderson? Sounds like an easy choice to me, but hey, I'm only God.

October 16

You cannot move away from something horrible because it will chase you all over hell and back. Unless your divorce lawyer gets you a restraining order.

October 19

If I expected you to be without fault, I would not have created spell check.

October 25

There are but three laws: Thought is creative; fear attracts like energy; and love is all there is. For a while I had a fourth law—never get the turkey pastrami at the Carnegie Deli—but that is technically more of a restaurant review. And with my cholesterol, I better learn to like the stuff.

October 28

A ll relationships are holy. But if that is true, how come Marv Albert pleaded guilty for consensual biting?

October 31

⋀

God's fun idea for a Halloween trick: If the neighborhood grouch stiffs your kids for candy, here's what to do. Put a Ping-Pong ball in his car's gas tank. He starts it up, drives about fifty yards before the suction pulls the ball down and it cuts off the gas supply. The car stalls. The suction stops and the ball refloats to the surface. He can then restart the car and drive another fifty yards until the entire process repeats itself.

November 1

God's tip of the day: If you drive a BMW or Mercedes, always check the mileage before you valet park it. Those bastards will use it to run errands while you're having dinner.

November 3

God's revised tip of the day: What the hell was I thinking on May 10? *Godfather II* is better than *Godfather I*. The way Coppola did the back and forth between De Niro and Pacino, brilliant. Although what the hell was he thinking with *Godfather III*? I tried to sit through it again the other night. Painful. His daughter is unwatchable. So let me say this— never get a sequel unless it's *Godfather II*.

November 5

⚹

Joy, truth and love may be interchangeable. So are the plots of *Home Alone 1* and *2*.

November 11

Nothing stays the same, nothing remains static. Except the ineptitude of the Los Angeles Clippers.

November 15

Ⳟⳟ

God's little insight: Every time a bell rings, an angel doesn't get its wings. It's just a bell, it has nothing to do with angels. Plus, angels don't even have wings. Would you want somebody three hundred years old flying up there with all that air traffic?

November 18

⋔

I have not given you commandments; they are more in the form of general guidelines. Legal says they're commandments because they contain the mandatory word "shall," but as a general rule, I try not to be a jerk about it. Other than the one "Thou shalt have no other God but me."

November 24

There is nothing you can't have if you choose it. Although security at the department stores may disagree.

November 27

/A\

Another one of the mysteries even I can't explain: What is that little thing on the neck of a turkey? The same thing is on Joan Collins's neck, and I don't know why it's there either.

November 30

God has his own space. So keep the hell out of it.

November 31

⁂

This is a perfect example of how you have the entire planet screwed up. My calendar has a November 31—yours doesn't. You know how you're always rushing about, ten minutes late for everything? Add it up over the year and it comes to about one day's worth of time. And here it is, November 31. So change your calendars. What are you thinking—you calculate 365 days a year based on some dead Roman farmers from five thousand years ago looking at the stars with a stick and some twine? Real smart! Get with it, people.

December 1

Of all the things I have tried to teach you, it is only important that you remember one: Buy low, sell high.

December 2

I tell you this: I am performing a miracle right now. And it is called Viagra.

December 3

You know my favorite miracle? Not the parting of the Red Sea, not the loaves and the fishes. My favorite miracle? Michael Jackson's wife getting pregnant. Took me two weeks. I let the whole west half of the Milky Way galaxy go to hell while I was working on it.

December 5

God's little insight: Uri Geller really doesn't bend spoons with his mind; it's a trick.

December 8

Good things come to those who wait, but better things come to pushy people who shove their way to the front of the line and get to pick first. It's not fair, it's just the way it is.

December 10

One of the mysteries even I can't explain: why anyone would want a partridge in a pear tree.

December 15

L ife is not like a box of chocolates. It's more like Nathan's hot dog—not as long as you think and full of nasty surprises. With a lot of heartburn toward the end.

December 23

⁂

If I am all knowing, how come I can never finish the *New York Times* crossword puzzle during lunch?

December 25

I don't know why, but I keep feeling I'm forgetting somebody's birthday. Jesus Christ, my mind must be slipping.

December 26

God's little insight: Those stars on the front cover of *Playboy* . . . they're a mailing distribution code, not a secret signal of how many times Hef had sex with the centerfold. Look, don't get me wrong, the guy is impressive as hell, but at seventy-two he is not doing the nasty with Miss December four times. I'll tell you this, with the life he's led, he's one guy who's going to be disappointed when he gets to heaven. You light a pipe once up here and the fire marshal is all over you.

December 28

J oy and sacredness do mix. Oil and water do not. And during this holiday season, neither do alcohol and mistletoe.

December 31

There are those who believe that God should provide his children with bells and whistles to prove that he exists. Like my whole life revolves around what you want. It's New Year's Eve. Give me some time off and we'll see if we can do better next year.

⇝ Special Bonus ⇜
Interview with God

an uncommon interview

As you could tell from the dates in this book, God and I did not have a conversation every day. We spoke on a regular basis, but took a break from each other every few days, especially in the summer when he liked to take long weekends. Other days, he would just check in but really had nothing on his mind.

We both realized, at the end of our year of dialogue, that there were blanks in the record, things he had not touched on but wanted to share. From my end, I was afraid that people would think I let God off easy. After all, I let him communicate his thoughts without trying to pin him down on specifics about himself, heaven and his view of the universe. From his end, he wanted the chance to clarify a few things; he also wanted to soften his image a bit. So I suggested a no-holds-barred interview.

After a few weeks of back-and-forth negotiations, we set the ground rules. He would submit to a final interview on the condition that I didn't try to interpret his meaning or paraphrase his words. No questions were submitted in advance; he reserved the right to go back and change any of his answers, but never exercised that option.

So, as a **special bonus,** I have decided to include my Interview with God. I think it shows a side of God that doesn't come through in *Heaven Talks Back.* In the give-and-take of the interview he lets his hair down; you see less of the Supreme Being and more of the hurting inner child. As he put it: "Just because people think I'm infallible doesn't mean I'm happy."

So read *Heaven Talks Back* to find out what God wants; in Interview with God, you find out who he really is. I'm quite proud of what follows, because in the age of celebrity interviews, who is a bigger celebrity than God?

The following interview took place on April 1, 1998.

JM: *If you were an animal or tree, what would it be?*

God: You're kidding right? You're interviewing the Supreme Being and you want to know what kind of animal I'd be?

If I wanted questions like that I would have gone on Barbara Walters. By the way, is she the one married to Alan Greenspan or is that Andrea Mitchell? I guess I should know that. Okay, the question is important to you, I'll answer it. If I were an animal I would be an owl because I'm so wise. Although I heard a great joke about dogs recently. I forget most of it, but it ends with the words "because they can." So the answer is, I would want to be an owl or a dog.

JM: *Does everyone go to heaven? Even evil people like Adolf Hitler?*

God: Like I'm supposed to let you into my home just because you repent at the end. There's a good idea—kill twenty million people and hope that an "I'm sorry" covers it. Somebody tell Jerry Falwell that's the stupidest thing I ever heard. Life on earth is not a dress rehearsal. Get it right and you go to heaven. Get it wrong and you don't. It's why I gave people free will and choice . . . but to be honest, keeping people out is a bureaucratic mess. Case histories, appeals, recommendations from people here who once knew them. It's way too political. Most cases are not cut-and-dried. Quite honestly, I let my assistants make the decisions and only step in when there's a problem. If I had to do it over again I would reinvent heaven. Cut out the bureaucracy. Let everyone in and keep the assholes all in one section.

JM: *Do you really help teams win big sporting events? Today's athletes credit you when they win.*

God: One hundred million galaxies, five hundred trillion stars, six quintillion planets and some overpaid spoiled pituitary freak in the NBA thinks I care whether he makes a foul shot with three seconds left. I'm lucky if I catch one game a year. Plus it wouldn't be fair if I helped—I'm in our office NCAA pool. I've never helped any team win. Okay, I admit it—just the '69 Mets.

JM: *What names do you like to be called?*

God: With friends I'll answer to just about anything except "homeboy." People call me Yahweh, Lord, the Father and Clapton.

JM: *What is heaven like?*

God: It's very nice. When you create the universe you pretty much have first call on where you want to live. Me, I like warm because my circulation isn't so good. From what I hear, heaven is like Miami except not quite so humid. October is the nicest month.

JM: *What do you consider your biggest mistake?*

God: Definitely the sixth commandment. I create two different genders, load them both up with hormones, throw them together on one tiny planet, invent alcohol so they can have office parties, then tell them they can't copulate freely. Never should have done the adultery commandment. It would have been much better having "Thou shall not smoke."

JM: *What do you do for fun?*

God: Off the record?

JM: *No, everything is on, remember our deal.*

God: I'm not sure I should let you know this because

some people may not be able to handle it. Okay, what the heck. You're my fun. Each of you is like a character on a giant video game. I move you around, I put you in different situations and keep playing with you until you get wiped out.

JM: *So does that mean we don't have free will?*

God: You have free will—it's just that I like to put up little barriers in front of you to see how you use it. For example, remember when you were back at Villanova, at that Lambda Chi Alpha party, June '74? Remember you were with a girl named Kelly? Went to Drexel. Good figure, not too bright. Remember how when she went to the bathroom and that hot blonde named Joyce put the moves on you? I did that. Just wanted to see how you'd react.

By the way, you did the right thing—take care of date number one while getting Joyce's phone number for later.

JM: *What motivated you to do this interview?*

God: Quite frankly, I wasn't so sure I wanted to go through with it. Almost pulled a Streisand at the last minute and claimed I had a bad back. But my people advised me to do this. They said it would help promote the book. For whatever reason, people want to know what makes me tick.

JM: *What does motivate you?*

God: At five billion years old, not much.

JM: *It seems from our conversations that you have a pretty liberal attitude toward sex.*

God: Once again, everyone is a genius in hindsight. I had the choice early on, sex as procreation or to clear up complexions. I went for procreation. Given all the people with pimples out there, it should have been more of a hygienic thing.

I'm all for sex. For procreation, recreation, whatever. You live what, six hundred years? Sorry, that's how long they live in the Alpha Centauri system. Let me check my files. Okay, humans live seventy years. Have some fun. Enjoy yourself. Have sex.

JM: *So you forgive Frank Gifford for what he did with that flight attendant.*

God: Forgive him! I helped set it up! After fifteen years with the Antichrist he deserved a night out.

JM: *Kathie Lee is the Antichrist?*

God: Okay, she's not the Antichrist. She's worse. At least the Antichrist isn't a hypocrite. With him, what you see is what you get. But her! She preaches charity and pays her workers twenty-three cents an hour, she talks about love but is completely intolerant of anyone who doesn't agree with her, she brags about her perfect kids and uses them for ratings. We're talking a minimum of thirty years of therapy until they become even remotely functional. Will somebody tell that woman that their bathroom habits are not a nationwide Kodak moment?

JM: *What did you think when you saw that famous* Time *magazine cover proclaiming that you were dead?*

God: I felt the same way Elvis feels whenever he reads that he's alive. You just gotta laugh.

JM: *At one point you talked about your "people." Could you tell us who they are?*

God: You get to a certain point, you become bigger than life. Michael Jackson has people, the queen has people, Sinatra had people. I have people. Not a whole entourage. Two or three PR types, a wardrobe person, a voice coach for when I speak and Bundini Brown. I just love hearing him tell me "you are the greatest."

JM: *Is it tough being God?*

God: You don't know the half of it. At least presidents have former presidents they can talk to. Who do I have? Nobody. There are no other Gods but me. I'm it. And last time I checked, there's nobody in line to help out.

JM: *Do you talk to the animals and can they talk back?*

God: Who do you think I am, Dr. Dolittle? No, I don't talk to the animals. And can you imagine if animals could talk? It's Richard Gere's worst nightmare.

JM: *How will we know when the end is near? Is it in the Book of Revelation?*

God: Actually it's in the Nielsens. The end will be near when the *Jerry Springer Show* is number one.

About the Author

Jon Macks, the man God has chosen to talk to, was bar mitzvahed in a conservative synagogue, then taught by Augustinian priests at Villanova University and Law School. As a result, he constantly hears three voices fighting in his head. Despite this, he is a writer for *The Tonight Show with Jay Leno,* has written the past two Academy Awards shows for host Billy Crystal, is a frequent contributor to *George* and has provided material for Whoopi Goldberg and Robin Williams at *Comic Relief.* Prior to his incarnation as a comedy writer, Macks was one of the nation's top political consultants. When not spending time in Los Angeles with his wife and three children, he punches up speeches for James Carville, John F. Kennedy Jr., Mary Matalin, Vice-President Al Gore and President Bill Clinton.